DOLPHINS SET I

FRESHWATER DOLPHINS

Megan M. Gunderson
ABDO Publishing Company

visit us at
www.abdopublishing.com

Published by ABDO Publishing Company, 8000 West 78th Street, Edina, Minnesota 55439. Copyright © 2011 by Abdo Consulting Group, Inc. International copyrights reserved in all countries. No part of this book may be reproduced in any form without written permission from the publisher. The Checkerboard Library™ is a trademark and logo of ABDO Publishing Company.

Printed in the United States of America, North Mankato, Minnesota.
042010
092010

 PRINTED ON RECYCLED PAPER

Cover Photo: Peter Arnold
Interior Photos: Corbis p. 17; © Kevin Schafer / SeaPics.com p. 8;
    Peter Arnold pp. 13, 14, 15, 18, 19; Photo Researchers p. 5; Photolibrary p. 21;
    Uko Gorter pp. 7, 9

Editor: Tamara L. Britton
Art Direction & Cover Design: Neil Klinepier

Library of Congress Cataloging-in-Publication Data

Gunderson, Megan M., 1981-
  Freshwater dolphins / Megan M. Gunderson.
      p. cm. -- (Dolphins)
  Includes index.
   ISBN 978-1-61613-413-6
   1. Dolphins--Juvenile literature. I. Title.
  QL737.C432G859 2010
   599.53'8--dc22
                                    2010001627

CONTENTS

FRESHWATER DOLPHINS

Freshwater dolphins are **cetaceans**, just like all other dolphins. All cetaceans are mammals. So, freshwater dolphins are **warm-blooded** and make milk for their babies. They must surface to breathe air above water.

Yet unlike most dolphins, freshwater dolphins live away from salty seawater. They live in rivers and lakes instead.

Many freshwater dolphins are found in South America and Asia. The Amazon river dolphin is a common freshwater dolphin. The Ganges, Indus, and Chinese river dolphins are other well-known freshwater dolphins.

The Amazon river dolphin's neck and skin bend easily. This allows it to swim effortlessly around trees and other obstacles.

SIZE, SHAPE, AND COLOR

A freshwater dolphin's size depends on its species. Amazon river dolphins are among the largest. They reach nearly nine feet (2.7 m) in length. Indus river dolphins are the shortest, reaching just over eight feet (2.5 m).

Chinese river dolphins are among the heaviest. They can weigh more than 530 pounds (240 kg)! Indus and Ganges river dolphins may weigh just 155 pounds (70 kg).

Most freshwater dolphins share features that set them apart from other dolphins. They often have broad flippers, rounded foreheads, long beaks, and small eyes. Their dorsal fins are small, too. Some simply look like a hump!

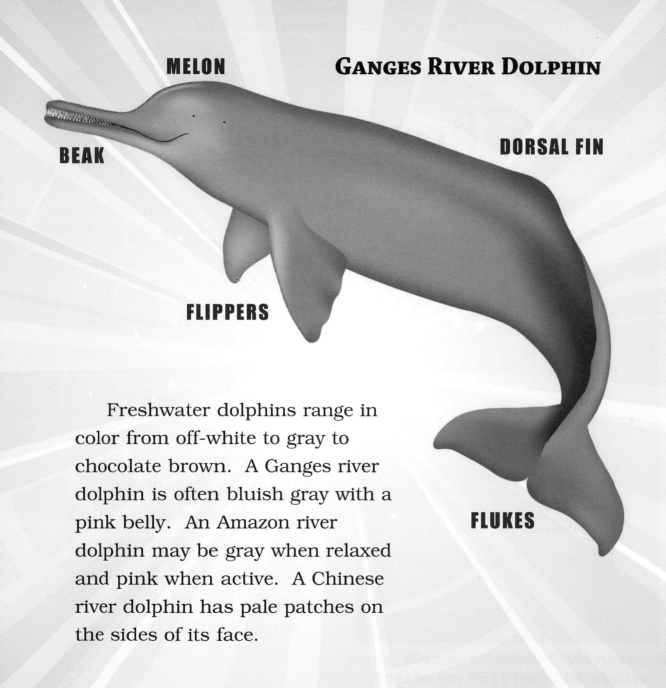

MELON

GANGES RIVER DOLPHIN

DORSAL FIN

BEAK

FLIPPERS

FLUKES

Freshwater dolphins range in color from off-white to gray to chocolate brown. A Ganges river dolphin is often bluish gray with a pink belly. An Amazon river dolphin may be gray when relaxed and pink when active. A Chinese river dolphin has pale patches on the sides of its face.

SENSES

A dolphin's senses allow it to survive in its **habitat**. Dolphins can taste their fishy food. But, scientists do not think they have a sense of smell.

Unlike most dolphins, those that live in rivers usually have poor eyesight. Yet scientists believe they do not need it in their dark, muddy homes.

Navigating through muddy river water is no problem for these dolphins. They simply rely on their sense of hearing. It is an important part of echolocation.

To use this system, a dolphin sends out a series of clicks. The clicks travel out through its **melon**. Then, the sounds bounce off any object in the dolphin's path. Those echoes return to the dolphin. They tell it the object's size, shape, distance, and speed.

River dolphins also have a keen sense of touch. They use their long beaks to poke into river bottoms. There, they find hidden prey.

Sound wave sent out by dolphin

Echo wave received by dolphin

DEFENSE

Freshwater dolphins are among the world's most **endangered** mammals. In fact, scientists think Chinese river dolphins are nearly extinct. Freshwater dolphins do not appear to have any natural predators. Humans are their main threat.

Freshwater dolphins cannot escape threats to their **habitats**. Agriculture, **deforestation**, and mining all take place around their river homes. These human activities cause water pollution.

Fishing also poses a threat. Freshwater dolphins may drown after becoming tangled in fishing gear. Ganges and Indus river dolphins have even been hunted for their meat.

Dams are another human-made danger. Freshwater dolphins often **migrate** throughout a river during seasonal flooding. Yet today, many dams block that normal movement. Dams also separate dolphins from their food sources.

Scientists fear it may be too late to save the Chinese river dolphin.

FOOD

A freshwater dolphin's **habitat** determines its prey. They all eat a variety of fish. Ganges and Indus river dolphins add shrimps to their diet. Amazon river dolphins will also snack on **mollusks**, **crustaceans**, and even small turtles.

The Ganges river dolphin's beak can grow more than 8 inches (21 cm) long.

Using echolocation, freshwater dolphins can find food in the cloudiest water. They also dig in river bottoms with their beaks to find food.

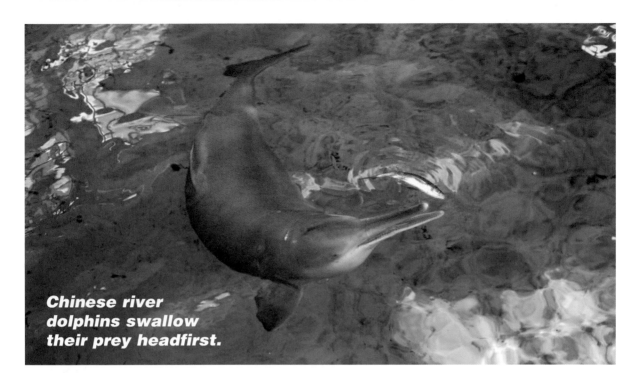

Chinese river dolphins swallow their prey headfirst.

Amazon river dolphins sometimes work together to trap prey against riverbanks. They will even steal from fishing nets for an easy meal!

Ganges and Indus river dolphins grab their prey with long, pointy teeth. Amazon river dolphins have special back teeth that help them crush prey. This allows them to eat armored catfish and other hard animals.

BABIES

A female freshwater dolphin may become **pregnant** after mating. Freshwater dolphins are pregnant for 10 to 12 months. They usually give birth to just one baby each time. It is called a calf.

Since dolphins are mammals, they make milk to feed their young. Freshwater calves will nurse for up to one year. But, some begin eating solid food at just two months old.

Freshwater dolphins have a range of life spans. Amazon river dolphins live the longest. They can survive up to 36 years.

Young Amazon river dolphins are gray. They become more pink to nearly white with age.

BEHAVIORS

Unlike ocean dolphins, freshwater dolphins do not gather in giant schools. More often, they live alone. Or, they are found in groups of up to ten individuals. When together, they communicate using a variety of whistles and other sounds.

Freshwater dolphins are also known for the **unique** noises they make above the water. When Amazon river dolphins breathe out

Ganges (above) **and Indus river dolphins are very similar. Some scientists believe they belong to a single species.**

through their blowholes, they sometimes make a loud sneezing sound. The Ganges river dolphin makes noise when it breathes out, too. This sounds like its nickname, susu!

Scientists continue to study these dolphins and their **unique** features. They hope to protect freshwater dolphins from future harm.

Amazon river dolphins may gather in small groups around food sources.

FRESHWATER DOLPHIN FACTS

Scientific Name:

Amazon river dolphin *Inia geoffrensis*

Chinese river dolphin *Lipotes vexillifer*

Ganges river dolphin *Platanista gangetica*

Indus river dolphin *Platanista minor*

Common Names:

Amazon river dolphin, boto, bufeo, pink dolphin

Chinese river dolphin, baiji

Ganges river dolphin, susu

Indus river dolphin, Indus susu

Average Size:

Freshwater dolphins reach lengths of eight to nine feet (2.5 to 2.7 m) depending on their species. Adults weigh between 155 and 530 pounds (70 and 240 kg).

Where They're Found:

In river systems in Asia and South America

GLOSSARY

basin - the land drained by a river and its connected streams.

cetacean (sih-TAY-shuhn) - a member of the order Cetacea. Mammals such as dolphins, whales, and porpoises are cetaceans.

crustacean (kruhs-TAY-shuhn) - any of a group of animals with a hard shell and jointed legs. Crabs, lobsters, and shrimps are all crustaceans.

deforestation - the act of removing trees and clearing forests.

endangered - in danger of becoming extinct.

habitat - a place where a living thing is naturally found.

melon - a rounded structure found in the forehead of some cetaceans.

migrate - to move from one place to another, often to find food.

mollusk - any of a group of animals with a soft body usually enclosed in a shell. Clams, snails, and squids are all mollusks.

pregnant - having one or more babies growing within the body.

unique - being the only one of its kind.

warm-blooded - having a body temperature that is not much affected by surrounding air or water.

WEB SITES

To learn more about freshwater dolphins, visit ABDO Publishing Company on the World Wide Web at **www.abdopublishing.com**. Web sites about freshwater dolphins are featured on our Book Links page. These links are routinely monitored and updated to provide the most current information available.

INDEX